a book of changes

is proud to present

Failing
your way
to success

A collection of inspirational
thoughts and poems

Written by
Steve Rock
the inspirational poet

Filament
Publishing

Filament Publishing

14, Croydon Road, Waddon,
Croydon, Surrey. CR0 4PA
+44 (0)208 688 2598
sales@filamentpublishing.com

Steve Rock is managed by
Elite Squad (Entertainment) Ltd
+44 (0)1403 871200
e-mail tony@elitesquad.freeserve.co.uk

Steve Rock asserts the moral right
to be identified as the author of this work.

Printed by Antony Rowe Ltd, Eastbourne
Editing - Tony Rock
Proof Reader - Anthony F. Germing
Deisgn and layout - Dave Fowler DNF Creative
Cover design - Jim Cooper www.ninedeuce.net
Photograph of Steve Rock by Joe Bangay

ISBN 0-9546531-4-9

What they say about Steve Rock.......

"Thought provoking and inspiring words of wisdom. This little book is one you will want to return to again and again."

Dorian Grant
MD of Change Consulting Ltd

"Failing Your Way To Success" defines how powerful words on a page can be. Steve offers a gift for life. This collection of writings is both thought provoking and life changing. This books is a guide to inner success and fulfilment. Should be read daily.

Rachel Ferdinand
Founder of Empower Me 2B Me
Workshops for Youth

"This is a life changing book that makes you stop, think and act more positively. Steve Rock's words make perfect sense in a world so confused. A book that should be read by everyone."

Ben Szymonik
MD of Nexas Ltd

"The Wordsmith, how true that title is. Steve's words are more than inspiring, more than moving. They have the ability to open you up to all of life's amazing possibilities. A read that will ignite your spirit, life your soul, and engage your being towards its true purpose."

Martin Boothe
Author of "The Power to Move for Success"

3

"This book is full of priceless words of wisdom that are written from the heart and soul. It will inspire you and provoke your life positively. Steve is blessed with a talent of writing and has failed his way to success - maybe you can too!"

**Reg Athwal - International speaker
and human potential expert.
Co-author of the No.1 best-selling
'Wake Up...Live the Life You Love' series**

"I've read Steve's book through three times and each time I find more depth and meaning to his words. His style is clear and simple, yet his poetry and prose often contain a profound wisdom. Key concepts about life, the universe and everything are summed up in short and sweet verse and some terrific one-liners. I've spent the best part of sixteen years studying the fighting and spiritual arts of the world, but Steve managed to blow me away with his elegant nutshell "Everyone and everything is a teacher". The Rock rules ok."

**Jan Storey, Author 'T'ai Chi - Stillness in Motion'
(StarDrum 2004)**

Sometimes you gotta create
what you want to be a part of.
- Geri Weitzman

Index of Contents

Foreword

Many people write that persistence is incompatible with failure, many other people know and live it every day, and none of them do so with more belief, passion and energy than Steve Rock.

The biggest challenge with this inspiring and sometimes uncomfortable idea, is communicating it with people in a way that they will not only understand, but in a way they will take it on board:

To increase their choices
To make them more aware of their possibilities
To open up new paths to success

Business books sit on shelves, unread. Conference speakers continue to bore people rigid with PowerPoint presentations and academic tomes continue to fill these messages with so much jargon, hype and mystery that most people simply turn away.

Steve brings inspirational prose and poetry alive and alight, his words seem to touch the hearts, minds and being of his readers.

He knows that peace, success and achievement are for everyone, not just a chosen few.

Through his words Steve helps to release our natural talent, genius and potential that is waiting to be unleashed. And when our potential is unleashed we discover who we are, why we are here, and then we start to live the life we were born to lead.

What you read in these pages will inspire you, make you think, and it will make you wonder, about life, about you, and about each other.

Enjoy that wonder - no-one else delivers it like Steve.

With love

David Taylor

Author of "The Naked Leader"
www.nakedleader.com

Dedicated to the part of you that will never give up and to all who make the time to read this.

Steve Rock

The inspirational poet and wordsmith for the 21st century, Steve Rock is a man that walks his talk; he firmly believes that dreams are meant for living and promotes this message through his writing and keynote speeches.

Steve has worked across the last 2 decades presenting and writing numerous shows for national television including CBBC and CITV. He holds workshops on creative writing nationwide with great success.

Steve also speaks at events for clients such as Her Majesty's Prison Service about success being a journey and not a destination.

He is an inspired author, speaker and poet. Steve produces monthly pieces of uplifting and thought-provoking writing which is now in circulation worldwide. Subscribers to the message are growing each day.

Steve Rock is the inspirational story teller for now and the future; his goal is to change the world piece by piece through collective and creative effort.

Steve Rock
The Inspirational Poet

a book of changes

therock@abookofchanges.com
www.abookofchanges.com

Photograph by Joe Bangay

Indomitable Spirit

Find a mirror.
Can you see the fire?
Look deeper.
Deeper still, feel life's unquenchable desire.

Your struggle to get this far,
has it been worth it?
To struggle is down to perception.
It matters not, for you have
the indomitable spirit.

Who the hell am I?

I'm a Wordsmith.
My life is simply words.
My religion is to live and die without regret.

I attempt to live my dreams and by you reading this means I have achieved another one. Thank you for assisting me.

When was the last time you had a dream and not worried about 'how' the dream was going to be achieved? When was the last time fear took hold of you, tied you up and paralysed you from trying something new?

I guarantee that you are not alone in feeling this - it seems to be part of the human condition.

Only you can make a better life for yourself. Many people may sell magic formulas and books to help guide you along the way, but when all is said and done, the ball truly is in your court.

We must take responsibility for our actions and understand with our soul that there isn't really any secret. The answers have always been and will always be inside of you.

The question is, do you really want to take the time to look?

This book is composed of some pieces that I wrote for myself in order to try to battle with some of my own demons. I'm not a guru or a leader of nations, I'm just a human, like you, trying to be the best I can possibly be and the method I use to do this is via the written and spoken word. If sharing a part of my soul helps one other person, then I'll allow myself a little smile.

If it doesn't help anyone else, then it's helped me, so either way, this process hasn't been in vain.

Fail again and fail better

We get so used to things in life breaking or smashing around us. Most possessions in our life are perishable; we almost expect nothing to last.

So when we get some bad news or something we're just not expecting, is it any wonder that we to behave like the belongings in our life - and breakdown.

I had a toy once, I think it was a touch-controlled car. (At the time it was considered state of the art machinery - given my age away now.) Anyway, I played with this toy all the time, there wasn't a place I wouldn't take it. I'm surprised it lasted as long as it did. Until one day I asked too much of it.

I took it into the woods and joined some of my friends who had set up a course for the toys we had. There were log jumps into rivers. (Well, they were puddles really, but I was so small that it may have well been a river.)

Over and under logs, down kerbs and into the road where real cars played. These toys took a real battering, so I shouldn't have been surprised when mine played chicken with a tree - and the tree won. I was devastated - my toy had broken down, it had come up against an obstacle that it just couldn't surmount.

I know that in my life I too have hit the largest obstacles and felt deep in my soul that my fight had left me, I had no more to give. But thankfully, unlike the toy car, our spirit is made of tougher stuff.

We are made of the right matter to get us through anything, if only we would try.

To quote Samuel Beckett, fail, fail again and fail better.

We have the ability to pick ourselves up and keep marching forward towards our goal. Our creative minds can answer any question we pose it, nothing need be unknown to us, and I truly believe this with every ounce of my being.

We are meant to succeed - we have an indomitable spirit. The question is, will you believe that you can do most things in life, or will you give up at the first hurdle saying "It was too hard," or "I'm just not lucky."

The same spirit that resides in you resided in the holy men of every generation. The same spirit that broke the three minute mile is the same spirit that helps you run to catch the bus, and the same spirit that enabled Nelson Mandela to survive in prison and come out and run his country is the very same spirit that gets you through schooling. You have fought off germs and illness, and you'll have more than a few 'battles' before you're through.

You are here now and no doubt have overcome many difficulties in your life already which proves me right, you have an indomitable spirit.

Days like these

Sitting back, thinking things.
When it rains it pours -
we all have days like these.
Want to laugh, instead you cry.
To find your happiness look deep inside.
In a job you love to hate
you're worth much more
be free of that place.
Battles to fight, will they ever stop?
Pick yourself up child and climb to the top.

Sitting back, thinking things
When it rains it pours -
we hate days like these.
A baby's smile can make us cry
reminds us of the good things
we have inside.

Days like these means happy to sad.
Cursing all the good luck you never had.
Wanting a change that never comes.
Can't take anymore.
Where are you going to run?

Days like these come and go.
Nothing lasts forever,
this you know.

Days like these are meant to be,
it makes me who I am
and you who you're supposed to be.

Don't be stupid!

It's Sunday morning, early May, I wake up feeling incredibly serene. The sun pokes its head through my slightly parted curtains washing me with a gentle heat. As I like to sleep with my window slightly open so air can circulate my room, I have made great friends with a bee I like to call 'Stupid'.

I call him "Stupid" because I couldn't understand how one creature, with the whole world to fly in, would get himself stuck on the inside of my bedroom window, and then proceed to panic when he couldn't find his way back into the big wide world.

At 8.30am, I hear the faint buzzing of my friend, Stupid. Once I would have reacted to the buzzing with great fear; after all, Stupid was put on this earth just to sting me. It couldn't possibly have any other interest, could it? As I stirred, I wondered what would happen if I didn't take my usual approach of trying to kill it.

So I lay still and have faith that the window nets will protect me from Stupid, or protect Stupid from me, depending on your point of view. I doze in and out of sleep for the next ten minutes and when I awake I realise there is a lack of frantic buzzing.

Maybe it's waiting for the right moment to strike, and maybe I'm dumb enough to assume that everything in this world is all about me. I edge stealthily out of bed. If Stupid was stalking me, I would now turn the tables.

To my amazement, after checking all possible hiding places, Stupid was nowhere to be found. By nature Stupid had found its way into my world and naturally, it had found its way out. Maybe Stupid wasn't so stupid after all.

Nature has the capability of providing the way, if we have faith, belief and give it time.

We only need to KNOW that the answers have always been around us, and always will be around us. Sometimes, in our haste and with our supposed intelligence we bang around, frantically in search of the 'answer'. Getting frustrated when the answer we want doesn't appear when we WANT it. After all, everything does revolve around us, doesn't it...?

A lady once said to me referring the sea: "Don't ever struggle or panic if you are caught in the ocean, because if you do the current will drag you down. You have a higher chance of survival if you keep calm and don't thrash about aimlessly."

This seems like common sense, yet when it comes to our everyday life, we do just the opposite. If the tide isn't going our way, we thrash, kick and scream, thinking this behaviour will get us what we want quicker. When in fact it can do just the opposite and carry us further away from the result we desire.

There are times to run, times to walk and times to contemplate.

Keeping still is also a form of action.

Listen

The light fills you from above,

but you find it hard to retain,

as quickly as it comes,

it seems to filter through

you once again.

Norman

Once upon a time there was a man who had no friends, no family. He didn't even have any pets. Let's say his name is Norman.

Norman's personality could be likened to a blank canvas, waiting for someone to splash a dash of colour on it. At the age of 20 he got a job and was very excited by this. He then fell into a crowd that was less than desirable. They drank - he drank. They smoked - he smoked. They stayed off work - Norman stayed off work. And so this went on.

A few weeks into his 'new' life, he decided that he was bored doing the same things as the others all the time. He decided that he wanted to become the owner of his own successful business. So he asked his friends for their advice but all they advised him of were the pitfalls...

It's at this stage that I would like to ask you a question. Why did Norman ask his 'friends' for advice?

Do you think Norman has the strength of character to be able to keep his friends and achieve his dreams and desires? Is he a leader, does he have the power of his own convictions? Do you believe that he may have to spend less time with his newfound friends in order to have half a chance of hitting his goal?

How many times have you tried to achieve things, while surrounding yourself with people who may love you but inadvertently knock your dreams, or aren't the most helpful? I'm not saying drop your life-long friends, but what I am saying, in order to learn how to fly, you may need to talk to some birds, if you get my meaning.

You may have to find the time to hang out with people who know about flying and know how to do it successfully. Sometimes we ask the opinions of people who mean well, but don't actually know any more than you about your chosen subject.

Let's get back to Norman. After 20 years of spending 90% of his time doing what the 'lads' do, it should come as no surprise that Norman found himself in a position where he had exactly what the 'lads' had. A beer belly that looked like he had swallowed a round-ish creature, whole! He was still in a job that he disliked, he had become 'comfortable' with his wage and he continued to spend it in unproductive ways!

Norman and his friends continually found fault with their employers, and the money they paid. The world was such a horrible place. Those who had a better life were labelled 'lucky' and that 'luck' was only reserved for a few fortunate people in the world. And so life went on for Norman until another 25 years had passed. On the verge of retirement he had witnessed a lot of his friends move away, pass away, or get married and have children.

Only one of his friends had a fairly stable financial situation, the majority were on, or just above, the poverty line.

Norman felt he had no choice in how his life turned out. This was how it was supposed to be...wasn't it?

If you leave fewer things to chance and gain control over your environment, what you do socially, whom you speak to, and what you speak about, you will find, as if by magic, that life could start to look very different indeed.

Don't be a Norman.

Live today

A child is born
with a free state of mind.
No expression of hate.

The heart is pure and kind.
They know 'now' is what matters
not 'then' or 'what's to come.'

Simple things make them happy,
they find beauty in the rising sun.

Time is in great demand.
A minute goes
but never comes back.

Nothing lasts forever,
we should never forget that.

When is now?

Okay, I have a question for you? I warn you in advance that this is no normal question. It's the kind of question that may have you pondering for some time to come. Then again, if you have more intelligence than I do, the answer may present itself with no trouble at all. Are you ready? Are you sitting down? Okay, here it is.

When is 'now'?
Was it just 'then' or is it yet to come?

When did you last really experience living in the now? The present. When did you last live fully in the moment? Have you ever really lived in the moment?

This means being totally aware of all things going on in and around you. Extracting pleasure from simply existing.

This means not thinking about the past, or what is to come, but NOW!

The closest most of us get to 'now' is when we're caught up in a daydream, thinking about nothing in particular. Remaining 'present' can easily increase the quality of your life.

Next time your partner/child/friend speaks to you, try giving them your undivided attention. Think about nothing else apart from the words that tumble from their mouths, listen to their tone, pay more attention as opposed to letting your brain meander off and think about what it is you have to do tomorrow, or what's on TV later that evening.

Have you ever experienced 'now' without distracting the mind with activities?
The smart among you will respond that you experience 'now' while sleeping, but alas, that doesn't count.

If you never have experienced the magical wonder that is your breath entering and leaving your body, you're missing out on one of the wonders of the universe.

I'm talking about allowing your brain to relax and unwind, to just 'be'.

In my opinion we spend too much time doing and not enough simply 'being'. You would never consider staying on a treadmill for the majority of the day for fear of fatiguing or injuring your muscles.

So why should your brain be any different?

When was the last time you really felt and appreciated the water pulsing out of the shower, or really heard the birds sing their cheerful song of life? When was the last time you submerged yourself in the simple joy of living?

I can already hear some of your thoughts. "Steve, it's all very good and well, but it's not very practical is it? I work in a high-powered job, or I have 17 children to look after, I have bills to pay, etc, etc, etc."

My response is simply this; all that responsibility, all those things you 'have' to do, simply won't get done effectively, if at all, if you don't stop once in a while and think about 'now' and allow yourself to just be.

In this day and age time has come to govern our lives, one hour for lunch, thirty minutes to get to work, forty five minutes before I pick up the children. There is one important mark missing on all time devices and that mark should simply read,

'Now'.

Banish all doubt

When the sun seems a distant memory,
don't you worry about a thing.
After the cold harsh winter
comes the light vibrant spring.
In the darkness of the soil
colours within the stem reach out.
From darkness comes light
to turn away the shadows of doubt.

In times of inner turmoil
due to outer confusion,
any words of negativity are
usually just an illusion.

Know who you are
and more importantly what you're about.
Because what you're made of within
will always triumph over the
seeds of self-doubt.

Moments

Each moment is a place you've never been.

Take your time and please read this statement again.

Each moment is a place you've never been.

Are you with me? Or are you sitting there thinking that I'm a mad man speaking double Dutch?

Each moment is a place you have never been simply because you physically can't recreate a moment in time. Something will always be different. It may be the weather, or how your heart is beating at that precise moment.

You may be eating something different on this occasion, or having different thoughts; or time has simply moved on, but this moment, right now, you have never lived before.

So why do we get hung up on past failures so often? We're so quick to remind ourselves of 'that time' when we didn't make the grade, or 'that time' when we were out of work.

Whatever the 'failure' is for you, it never lasts and is no indication of what is to come. Each moment is new.

Your past doesn't necessarily mean your future. We can re-design our future at will. Don't allow the shackles of the past to hold you back.

The most beautiful thing in the world

The most beautiful thing

in the world

is the world itself.

And you are part of the world.

You are already Perfect

What are you looking for when you go to the store and spend money that you may not have? Who are you trying to kid when you go to the car showroom and see a car you can't quite afford, but the little voice in your head says, "People will think better of you." Who are you trying to impress?

The big house, the fancy holidays, the expensive jewellery, all these things will carry much more value if you truly viewed YOURSELF as the priceless possession.

You are already perfect.

I do believe that financial wealth is something worth striving for, as long as you understand that it is the icing on the cake and not the cake itself.

In today's world money does serve a purpose, but so does your spirit.

And too often I come across so many people who are geared up just for financial wealth and neglect the feeling that spiritual wealth can bring.

If only we could attain balance.

We place such a high value on things money can buy, and neglect to see that the real value can be found in the things that we are given for free.

Life.

If we have the misfortune of bumping our vehicle, we can replace it. If our home gets broken into and some of our material belongings get taken, while annoying, we can replace those too.

But have you tried replacing your life? Without which, the car and the home have no meaning.

You are already perfect.

When was the last time you looked into your partner's eyes and was awestruck? Nobody in the world has eyes like him or her.

Your partner, family, friends are all original pieces of art that should be marvelled at every day.

We get so used to seeing 'expensive' art in frames, that we forget to notice the priceless art that is all around us.

You are already perfect.

When was the last time you thought about how your heart keeps pumping blood around your body?

Your heart is made of a special type of muscle that doesn't become fatigued. Each heartbeat that we feel in our chest is one complete contraction and relaxation of the heart muscle.

Your heart is the engine that keeps your body going.

Every day this vital organ beats about 100,000 times, pumping the equivalent of 2,000 gallons of blood...
and you don't even think about it!

You see, I'm right. You are already perfect.

If this is something you can do without 'thinking', imagine the things you can do when you set your mind to achieving a particular result.

The cars, the homes, the high-powered jobs, the expensive clothes and jewellery are great. Just don't put too much emphasis on them.

For if you make these things the reason for WHO you are, then what happens if you lose them?

Do you not risk losing yourself in the process?

Why risk that when you are already perfect?

Stretch

Sometimes in life we have to
strive for something,
that at first may seem
a little out of reach.
But in time,
with persistence,
the thing
that once was impossible
becomes a reality
and this experience
will enable us to teach.

A single event

A single event can shape the rest of your life.
From waking up later,
to going for a swim with
the rising of the sun,
or neglecting the reading of the paper.

To change just one thing
can change your entire life destination.
Taking a job you don't really want,
to maintaining a relationship
you know isn't right.

The pages of your story are written
day by day,
take full responsibility for your actions.
This is your chance to write the perfect book
why would you want to give that
opportunity away?

The 'F' word

No matter how good a person we are, we all associate with the 'F' word.

Do you remember while being taught at school, anyone who said the 'F' word would be in some serious trouble? Even at home, while chewing on some wholesome food, if you ate something that was too hot for the delicate membrane in your mouth and the 'F' word slipped out, all hell was to be paid. Well, it was in my house anyway.

I recall an incident when I was growing up. What am I talking about? I still am growing up! Anyway, I was in my senior year at school, minding my own business, when I saw two boys squaring up just outside the school gates.

They looked mad as hell. So obviously, as opposed to stopping this war, everyone formed a circle and started chanting "Fight, fight, fight". Before long the entire year was there, waiting for the first sight of blood.

These two giants of men (anything taller than me was given the 'giant' status), stood eyeballing each other and then it started.

No, nobody threw a punch but a tirade of abuse flew from each of their mouths. "You F'ing *%!* You can F right off...you mutha F'er!" And so it continued, until the headmaster appeared on the scene and handed out 1000 lines to each of them, the repeated line was to be "I shall use clean language at all times".

The 'F' word can get us into all sorts of trouble, young and old. There are times when we should avoid using it, and there are times when some people would argue that we should use it.

But there is another 'F' word that carries with it much more danger. This 'F' word causes more damage than we could ever imagine.

We associate all kinds of terrible things with this word. With it comes low self-esteem, low confidence, and insecurity on a massive scale. And yet this 'F' word isn't half as notorious as the other 'F' word of which we spoke.

As we get older we are taught to avoid this 'F' word at all costs; which means that, more times than not we cease to even try something in fear of coming face to face with it.

The comforting thing is, the majority of successful people learn to deal with this 'F' word; they learn to understand it as part of a greater process that will ultimately carry them to where they're aiming to be.

These people don't run from this word, they have an understanding of it. They know that nothing in life can be achieved without the help of this word, and so we should all learn and understand this. Those clever sods among you will have already guessed the word.

Failure

Nothing of any worth has ever been achieved
without coming face to face with 'failure'

No chef has ever baked a cake without
making a few mistakes.

No 100-metre runner has ever won a race
without losing a few first.

No child has ever learnt to walk,
without first stumbling a few times.

As we age we get fearful, a touch embarrassed
if we aren't seen to be perfect at all times.

Well, I've got news for you, your perfection
includes all of your failures as well.

You gotta break a few eggs to make an
omelette as they say.

Everyone and everything is a teacher.

Sometimes - part one

Sometimes, not all the time,

I want to give in.

Sometimes, just sometimes

I know I can fight anything and win.

Sometimes, sometimes

I feel completely blessed.

Sometimes, most of the time

I feel completely stressed.

Sometimes, just sometimes

I question my own ability.

Sometimes, NO, all the time

I must believe more in ME.

Your thoughts shape your life

Your life is shaped by two things. The kind of questions you consistently ask yourself and the meaning you give to the things that happen to you. We can never control all circumstances, but we can control what they mean, or how we interpret them.

This coming year, promise yourself to ask a better quality of question You will be surprised by the kind of answers your brain delivers if only you change your level of self-talk.

For instance, if you have just come from a painful relationship, don't ask yourself, "Why oh why does she/he hate me?". Your mind will answer, "Because you're an irrational jealous pig." Not that inspiring is it?

Try asking yourself a question like, "How can I learn and grow from this experience to benefit me in my future relationships?"

A better question will yield a better answer. Or, if you have been made redundant, the pre-programmed automatic response tends to be, "Poor me, why do I get all the bad luck? Why is life such a big pile of..."
Ask and you shall receive.

If you could just catch yourself and try asking instead "What opportunity is now open to me? What is the dream that I've been putting off for tomorrow? How can I now become the person I have always dreamed of being?" A higher quality question will deliver a higher quality answer; it's that simple.

Nelson Mandela was imprisoned for a large chunk of his life and nobody would've blamed him for wanting to physically assault the people who took away the prime years of his life. Why didn't he come out bitter and twisted like most people?

Could it be because he viewed prison as an opportunity to develop himself and a chance to show the world what he stood for?

Upon his release this man ruled the same country that had imprisoned him. Nelson Mandela controlled what he thought; he is a human being just like you and I. We have the same tools, the same ability to take control of our thoughts. So why are we so eager to hand over the controls to someone else?

The trouble is we are a society that has been trained to respond in certain ways when the fact is we have a choice about how we choose to react.

I have a mission for you, if you choose to accept it - next time you feel yourself losing your temper, slam the mental brakes on, and take control. Decide how you WANT to react and don't just let your previous programming take over.

If we can change how we think, then we can change our entire lives; after all, we are what we think. We usually focus on one thing at a time, so why not make that one thing positive?

Life

"I'm here for but a minute."
The young person said.
"I must use this minute wisely
and not be misled."

"I'm here for but a minute."
The young person reminded.
"I must use this minute wisely
and never be undecided."

"I'm here for but a minute."
The young person casually spoke.
"I must use this minute wisely
time is my commodity - I shan't
end up broke."

"I'm here for but a minute."
The young person had promised.
"73 years had passed
and I haven't even noticed."

"You're here for but a minute."
A ghostly figure said.
"Don't spend too much time talking
before you know it, you'll be dead."

How long do you have?

There have been times in my life when I was convinced that I really wanted to do something. I spend a lot of time researching and talking, but when it comes to 'doing', well, this is where the excuses start popping up, left, right and centre. Two of my favourite excuses are,

"It'll take too long", or "I don't have the time."

Now, these phrases have always aroused my curiosity. How long is too long? How much time do I expect? The bottom line is if I really wanted to do it then I would find the time. Don't lie to yourself; if you don't want to do something admit that it's just not the most important thing in your life right now. Nobody will tell you off. (Unless you're employed and are talking to your boss.)

Sometimes we may set a goal, then look at how long it'll take to achieve it and try to pull out; providing excuses in abundance rather than focusing on the positive feeling achieving the goal may provide.

The problem is that we live in an instant gratification society. We look at too many things as unachievable, simply because we fail to see, or have the 'patience', to arrive at the end result.

There are microwaves to make instant food to go with our instant coffee, we have instant communications, we want instant fame and instant wealth.

We're so eager rushing around, moving from one project to the next that we very rarely stop and smell the roses, or notice that the tree in the garden is just that tiny bit taller than it was last year.

In my opinion, anything worth achieving, may just be worth having the patience for.

For example, a man was told he would never be able to fend for himself, let alone walk again. This man was completely dependant upon others for EVERYTHING.

But he set himself a goal, a goal that he TRULY believed he could achieve.

The goal was 'simply' to finish the London marathon. It took six days for him to complete the course, but he did achieve his goal. If it had taken seventeen days would we have thought any less of his achievement?

I think not. For he was brave enough to have a goal and proceed towards it with an unshakable faith.

Next time you're about to complain about how long something may take you to achieve, remember that the time will pass anyway, whether we do the activity or not. Time doesn't care, it'll move on regardless of what you choose to do.

It doesn't matter how long it takes - just as long as you get there.

Remember

Think; listen,

before you act.

Act from a position of faith

and not desperation.

Desperation leads

to rushed

decisions.

Decisions should

never be rushed.

A story?

He was very good and playing very bad,
a middle class brother, knew how to keep
quiet 'bout the 'tings' he would have.

Always trying to win, or be in favour,
wanting to be respected and loved by his
own culture.

Brought up in a different situation,
at school he was only one of two from his
own nation.

The older he got, the more confused he
would become; the person he always thought
he was started to implode.

A growing experience had now begun.

Once a boy - reaching for his Mother's
apron strings, now a man - scared of what
maturity would bring.

Laughing in the times when he really wanted
to cry, all of his friends had no idea he was
slowly dying inside.

Walking the streets of life in search of a
different answer, it's more about the type of
question you ask, that's what really matters.

Spending hours alone, pondering on how he
ended up here.

Hours turned to days, and when nobody
missed him, he felt nobody cared.

One day, while staring into space,
sitting at his oblong prison.
A glimmer of hope sprung into his head,
he was one of God's own children.

With this in mind, he confidently typed
out his resignation, no longer would
he chase money, and take jobs out of
sheer desperation.

As he walked out through the revolving doors
for the last time, he knew that from this
moment on Life would work out just fine.

What is your life spec?

What do you think makes us feel fulfilled after a day at work? Could it be that we have completed a list of tasks that our job requires of us and our job spec has been satisfied?

Is it any wonder that we sometimes go through life feeling a bit lost, with no direction? Some people get home from a hard day at work and all they want to do is sit and watch TV allowing precious, never to be recovered time pass them by.

If we don't have a daily purpose that guides and inspires us and we continue to allow circumstances to lead us around by the tail, how are we ever going to feel good about ourselves and feel that uplifting sense of achievement?

We need to contribute to our daily good.

The reason we feel a sense of achievement when completing tasks at work is simply because they WERE SET in the first instance. We adhere to our JOB SPEC every working day and yet we never spend the time to create something far more important ...our LIFE SPEC! What is your Life Spec?

Who are you and more importantly, who do you want to be? Nobody has ever hit a target they can't see. If we don't know where we are heading, how will we recognize it when we get there?

Why is it that we can spend months planning a holiday, but when it comes to planning our lives we can never find the time? There always seems to be a million better things to do; like sleeping, washing up or painting the spare room. We spend more time arranging the breaks in our lives, than LIFE itself.

Here is a challenge for you. Spend half an hour, today, to write down some thoughts around what you think your Life Spec is, or should be. Are you that compassionate person you want to be?

Do you spend enough time looking after your health for optimum balance?

Do you spend more than you save? What are the small steps you can take to ensure an exciting, uplifting future?

I know that some of you may be thinking, "Steve, I don't have the time to do that, I've got to watch Eastenders at 7.30". Will missing a TV show have a dramatic effect on your life?

I know that NOT spending quality time discovering the person you want to be and uncovering the things in life you really want to do WILL have a dramatic effect on your life.

One day you will look back and think,
"What happened to Life?".

You may even end up cursing your luck.
Keep in mind that it may not be the luck
you should be cursing, but yourself.

Be all that you can be...and more.

1.10am

What's scaring you?
What is it you fear?
The answers you seek are not far,
open your heart and see they're near.

Where you are is not a place you have to
be, your future is not yet written in stone.
I promise if you make different choices,
the future is a place your soul will love
to roam.

How you spend your hours, minutes and
seconds is down to you.
But those hours, minutes and seconds,
once they're gone, they're gone for good.

Now's the time to paint and live a picture
of the future you want to see, pick and choose
the brightest colours for you are one of
nature's wonders, fly, as you're already free.

No man is an Island

This was a statement I took some time getting my head around. Who knows, maybe you were brighter than me at school and got this first time, but for me, I needed to take some time.

My time at school was largely spent wishing I was somebody else, somebody more famous, somebody more glamorous, somebody, well, less like me.

I was obsessed with being the 'star' football player, or the lead singer in a world famous group as I felt that's the person who made it all happen, on their own and I wanted the adulation that they were receiving.

I'm now going to put my neck on the line and risk a barrage of comments from incredibly 'successful' people. (Assuming they're reading this book.)

BUT, no 'successful' person became a success by themselves...ever.

Allow me to elaborate on this - everyone at some point had or needed some help. Now the help could've come in encouraging or discouraging words someone uttered; or it may have arrived in the shape of financial aid, or a friend may have even given just a look, but somewhere along the line, people require help in some shape or form.

When we work together and utilise each other's talents, success tends to be found a little quicker as opposed to trying by yourself.

Now some of you may get sad or depressed and say - "That's all very well Steve, but my friends can't help me as they have no clue about how to achieve the things I want."

This may be true, but never count them out;
do you think that it's possible that one of
your friends may know someone, who knows
someone who could help you?

How will you ever know if you don't do
something that once came as natural to you
as breathing... and ask a question?

The older we get the more insular and afraid
of asking questions we become. Somewhere in
our past we thought that asking questions
meant that we were weak. Well it's not! It's a
form of strength, for only when you know
your weaknesses can you do something about
them.

Most people in life actually really want to
help, the thing is, very few people actually
have the balls to ask. So next time you're
faced with a situation you are having diffi-
culty overcoming, look to the person closest
to you and ask if they could help...if they
can't then you've lost nothing, but if they
can, imagine where you could end up...

The Race

It was a race - much like any other race.
Some were fitter than others.
Some had better muscle definition.
Some had no muscle at all.

The clothes they wore didn't always look
right. Some looked quite out of place,
while others, well, they looked quite fetching.
This race was made up of both sexes, but
women didn't always get a fair draw.

In this race everybody wanted to win.
Such was their desire, they often trod over,
and in some cases on those closest to them.
How sad. How very sad.

They always thought it was their
exclusive right to win. To be king of the
castle- top of the heap by any means
necessary. It just didn't seem to matter who
was there before them, nor how they fell.

On the 11th day of the 9th month, the race seemed to be reaching a disastrous conclusion.

Alas, undone by their own stupidity, it brings tears to my eyes.

In this race they've been running against, fighting against and simply having all round conflict with themselves.

If the race continues in this way there can only be losers, and all will have the same name.

First name human.

Second name race.

A letter to you

What if I told you that you are the miracle?

What if I told you not to look for
changes in the outside world
- not before you made them inside first.

What if I told you that despite all
the questions that there was ever only
one answer.

You.

What if I told you that if you pay
attention to the small things in the world
you would never have any of the 'big'
things to worry over.

What if I told you that comfort could
be found in taking action?
What if I told you that it's okay to cry.
What if I told you that 'God' has always
and will continue to be inside.

Well, I am.

Your story

Once upon a time there was a gathering of hundreds of thousands of souls, all of which were hustling and bustling, shoulder to shoulder standing together. The weather was neither warm nor was it cold; it just, was.

As you stand in the centre of this melee you look around and decide that everyone looks familiar and yet no one looks the same. You suddenly feel a gentle surge of warm confidence flow through your body, something inside you lets you know that everything is going to work out fine. Out of these thousands of souls, you just know that this is your time.

More seem to join the gathering throng as you feel physically lifted from one place to the next. The sense of excitement fills the area as a surge of power is released and every single soul instantly seems to buzz simultaneously into the darkness that awaits them.

It takes a while to adjust to this mass movement but in no time you're effortlessly picking your way through the crowd.
The crowd are all heading to the same place, all of them have one job in mind.
Fertilisation.

You move from the back, stumble into the middle of the crowd and before you know it you're in the leading batch. You can see a few more bodies in front of you that you have to pass in order to get into pole position.

You don't panic, as you just know that no matter what happens, whoever is currently in first place won't be there for long. Now you occupy the front spot, you're leading in a contest you didn't even ask to enter and this contest is to be the most important contest in your life, this contest decides your life; if you don't win this contest, well, quite simply, you won't have a life.

You know how this story ends as you are here, you won the first race you ever entered, you're a winner from day one, you've already done the hard part, take comfort in knowing that the rest is relatively easy now.

The Voyager

I am the Voyager.
Exploring the depths of one's Soul
In search of reasons for my behaviour.
Predictable?
Much like the changing of the seasons.
I am the Voyager.
Prompting a response
- challenging the status quo
After all, what do they really know?

We spend too much time focusing
on our weakness.
We must encourage and
celebrate our uniqueness.
Living like clones.
We are square pegs trying to fit
into round holes
We aren't all chasing the same
dream and goals.
So much, so much time wasted
trying to unravel a mystery that
was never ever there.
Life.

You share your confusion with some who
don't even care.

No, no, no more skulking shoulders
hunching in the shadows.
Come forth into the light
know that not only can you pick
but WIN your own life fights.
I am the Voyager
Holding the lantern high.
This shining beacon is not that bright,
Trust, fear not, open your eyes.
Admire the view that projects
from within you.
It's there for a reason, much like those
ever changing of the seasons.

Now is the right time and the right place
Face yourself, you are no disgrace.
Stand tall my Child of God,
my follower of Light
My Sister, my Brother.
You have the foresight, the vision,
Have faith, people do want to listen.
Stop from being a follower and know that

YOU are the Voyager

Focus

Change of focus is a powerful thing.
A very powerful thing indeed.

When a business deal goes sour you could
do one of two things. Choose to focus on the
negative emotion and how hard done by you
are, or you could choose to change your focus,
control your state of mind and figure out
what you DO have control over and pour your
energy and emotion into that instead.
There is such a fine line between these two it's
almost invisible.   I said almost.

I recently had an experience where in one
phone call I lost the possibility of working on
a deal worth £20k. How do you think I felt?
Well if you can't guess, allow me to share
with you my emotion.

Gutted.

After kicking in the defenceless wall,
I calmed down and tried to gain control of
my thoughts.

I repeated, "I can't control all events, but I can always control my mental state."

With that in mind I went downstairs and watched the extras on 'The Lord Of The Rings' DVD.

For the next two hours I submerged myself in admiration for the author, the director and the actors who bought this masterpiece together.

While listening to some of the classic English actors interviewed, I thought to myself, "I want to get voice training. I want to sound as rich as that."

I proceeded to get on the Internet in search of as many links to Voice Coaching as possible. I came up with a couple of numbers to call the following morning as it was getting late. (I do need my beauty sleep.)

The next day I was on the phone. Soon I was speaking to this amazing individual who was as excited about life as I was and his professional credentials were second to none.

Not only did I get a wonderful deal, but also I felt deep in my soul that I have made a professional and who knows, maybe a personal friendship that will reap benefits beyond my wildest dreams.

I have my first two-hour coaching session next week and there are many possible business avenues we have to discuss as well.

The reason I have told you this short story is to show that not all bad news is, well, bad news.

If it wasn't for two things, the supposed 'bad' news and my awareness that focusing on the collapsed business deal couldn't help me get any closer towards my ultimate goal, then I would never have watched 'Lord of The Rings' and got inspired by something as simple as the clarity and richness of an actor's voice, which in turn led to the foretold sequence of events; and who knows where this meeting may lead me...

Sometimes Opportunity comes dressed as bad news and is hoping you will recognize her under her convincing fancy dress.

Some things in life aren't always what they first seem.

U can change

Who said life was easy?
Must live through hard times.
Answers are all around you.
Learn to read the signs.
Live your life today.
Have no trust in tomorrow.
Focus on the good things.
Have little time for sorrow.

We're born.
We then become.
What we become,
is down to us.

U Can Change.

To be restricted by other's perceptions
is foolish.
You determine what you can do.
Now the question is:
Do you have what it takes?

We are all hampered by circumstance.
Some use it is as a reason not to succeed.
Others use it as motivation to succeed.

A man called Emerson once said:
"Make the most of yourself,
for that is all there is to you."

U Can Change

GET UP!!

Get up, and climb the highest peaks,
the ones you dream of conquering
while you are asleep

It's your time to hunt all the possibilities
while others spend their time too
fearful to even seek.

Your scope is so vast,
your potential knows no ends.
Just find a dream that will last
this is the least you owe to yourself ,
my friend.

Get up - know that you ARE great!
Trying to plan your perfect entrance
time is a precious commodity
- why do you procrastinate?
The more you live, truly live,
the more you'll learn.

Living is more than being mundane
and focusing on how much you can earn.

Get up - for life happens 'now'
Life doesn't happen 'when.'

Too much time spent talking
will only lead to a regrettable end.

It's time to Get Up,
break free from the shackles
of uncertainty.

Now is your time and the place
to be the greatest human
that you possibly can be.

The first rule is to keep
an untroubled spirit.

The second is to look things
in the face and know them
for what they really are.

- Marcus Aurelius

Thank you for taking the time to read these poems and thoughts, I hope that you found one or more pieces that not only moved you, but moved you enough to take action in a specific area in your own life.

I look forward to sharing my journey with you again sometime soon.

Peace and love

Steve

Please visit

a book of changes

www.abookofchanges.com
for information on books and audio
programmes created by Steve Rock.

You can email Steve at
therock@abookofchanges.com

or write to

Steve Rock
c/o Elite Squad Entertainments,
Valtony, Loxwood Road,
Plaistow, West Sussex,
RH14 0NY, England

Thank you.

Steve's thoughts can also be found on
www.echievers.com